DEAR BLACK GIRL,

Can We Talk?

LOLITA E. WALKER

Illustrated by Aspen Walker

First Printing: 2023
ISBN: 978-1-7327928-8-3
Library of Congress Control Number: 2023908677

Published by Lolita E. Walker / Walker & Walker Enterprises, LLC.
16405 Livingston Road
Accokeek, MD. 20607
https://www.lolitawalker.com

Previous Works:
The Intersection of You & Change
Copyright © 2018 by Lolita E. Walker

Can We Talk? Letters & Poems to Reclaim a Bolder You
Copyright © 2022 by Lolita E. Walker

Dear Anxiousness, Can We Talk?
Copyright © 2023 by Lolita E. Walker

Ordering Information:

Special discounts are available on quantity purchases by corporations, associations, educators, and the general public.

For details, contact the publisher at the above-listed address.

U.S. trade bookstores and wholesalers: Please contact Walker & Walker Enterprises, LLC. Tel: (443) 353-9121 or email info@lolitawalker.com

WALKER & WALKER
E N T E R P R I S E S

2023

Dear Reader,
Can we talk?

THIS IS THE BOOK that every black girl should have on her nightstand.

I am a black girl who was raised by generations of black women. I remember from the time I was young; I was being groomed for greatness. My parents affirmed me before I understood what that meant. It was, therefore, surprising to me that the words that came out of the mouths of so many others, whether 12 years old or 112 years young, were not always as positive. I vividly remember my 5th-grade teacher, Mrs. Vera Smith, at Mary Church Terrell Elementary School in Washington, DC, telling me that I will go on to do great things because she saw the leader in me. Sometimes, it only takes one person to believe in you despite the circumstances that may cloud your way.

Whether it was because the media didn't always depict the amazingness that we gifted to the world or everyone's parents and community weren't as rich in words as mine or simply that our environment or circumstances prompted us to think that "more" for us was unreachable, this book is a shout-out that, *Dear Black Girl,* you are the greatness that others have yet to see.

This book is a reminder that the road will not be always easy, but through trials and tribulations, through ups and downs, and through celebrations and losses, we have the power to put words to the emotions that we experience daily. This book is a reminder that speaking with your inner self can help recolor and reshape the narrative of who it is that you think you are.

If no one has told you today, *Dear Black Girl,* you are God's gift to this world.

Dear Black Girl, **this book will empower you - and your inner critic too.**

Dear Reader,
Can we talk?

This is to you, from me.
I love you,

Lolita

BLACK GIRL MAGIC

or #blackgirlmagic [blak gurl **maj**-ik]

Black Girl Magic and #blackgirlmagic were created to celebrate the accomplishments and general amazingness of black women.

It is used as an expression of positivity and empowerment.

---

https://www.dictionary.com/

THE DEDICATION

This is dedicated to Aspen Walker, the book's 17-year-old illustrator, who used her God-gifted talent to bring my words to life.

I remember the day I first saw Aspen's artwork on social media.
It was breathtaking.
It was unique.
Each piece pulled me in.

As I stared at the intricacies within each detail, I could feel the emotions within the story that was being told. I remember wondering, does this *Dear Black Girl* know how much amazing talent is within her? Does she recognize that her work has the power to shift a person? A nation?

I couldn't believe that my niece had such a creative expression. I remember clicking the notifications for her new social posts and being in awe at the magic that came through each piece. I remember calling Aspen and sharing with her that I could envision her artwork as the cover of a book. I don't know if she believed me at the time, but through this book, I am elated to be a part of her journey.

Aspen, I am so proud of you. May this book remind you that you are limitless, with immense amounts of untapped potential. May holding this book in your hand be a reminder that there is someone around the world holding your book and your art is helping them to remember *Dear Black Girl,* I am you and you are me!

THE CONTENTS

THE FOREWORD

Dr. Juanita Miller, Former Maryland State Delegate, Former Chair of the Prince George's County Board of Education, Former Educator, Community Leader, and Activist.

Being black and female often comes with a multitude of life hindrances and obstacles. Whether you are from an upper, middle, or disadvantaged class, you will be confronted with greater obstacles at various levels than those in the "non-black, privileged" class.

Lolita E. Walker's poem, *"Dear Black Girl"* takes you there. Her words helped me recall the time I started my journey for a doctoral degree at a certain ivy league university. I was the only black female in my classes. Yes, I felt a little anxious and somewhat intimidated but I moved forward by working diligently to excel. I wasn't receiving the grades that I knew I had earned, so I left and enrolled in another more liberal university, where I was heard, seen, and respected. I earned my doctoral degree with flying colors.

Then there was the incident where I was next in line to be promoted to an administrative position upon my supervisor's pending retirement. I met all the criteria and qualifications for the position but that supervisor did everything to block it, even delaying her exit date!

In Lolita's book, she has a stanza that says, *"Dear Black Girl, you look ahead and only see obstacles of life that have mounted before you, before me…. but you did not fall."* Well let's talk because I believe and trust that what doesn't kill you makes you stronger. Stand a little taller, *Dear Black Girl!*

By the way, I didn't get that promotion but I did get elected delegate to the Maryland General Assembly and came in first place! This was an even bigger accomplishment than the administrative promotion! The election win personified the stanza in the poem that says, *"Unleashed like a beautiful beast who will soar higher and further and farther than even you can imagine."* Many more doors of opportunity opened for me after that. I was even cited in a publication for my leadership. At 76 years young, I still continue to soar!

Dear Black Girl, "You gain strength from your faith" and ride on the shoulders of *"your ancestors [who] will continue to lift you higher."*

I'm sure that Ms. Walker may have experienced similar situations, thus igniting the flame to have the poetic conversation in this book, *"Dear Black Girl, Can We Talk?"*

Dear Black Girl, I wish you much success in all that your heart desires! Continue having conversations as I do with Me, Myself, and God! This time, with you, yourself and God!

I conclude with a scripture that I read as a *Dear Black Girl, "Hope deferred makes the heart sick, but a longing fulfilled is a tree of life."—Proverbs 13:12*

THE COMMITMENT

***There will be times, while reading this poem, you feel as if you are in an uncomfortable hot seat. Please know that this is normal and you are not alone. Consider these moments as reflections that have the power to unlock different pieces of you that were simply waiting to be unleashed.

May you give yourself permission to soar!

My Commitment to You

I, Lolita E. Walker, will journey with you through this book.

Your Commitment to You

I _____, (insert your name) on the date of _____, am committed to giving myself space to read, reflect, and feel the power within this pause. I commit to allowing these words to penetrate areas that may not yet be uncovered or unleashed within me. I commit to gifting myself all of me.

Signed: _____

Dear Black Girl,

Can We Talk?

WALKER & WALKER
E N T E R P R I S E S

2023

www.lolitawalker.com

Dear Black Girl,

You may have shown up today
with a heavy heart and a troubled disposition.

You may have doubt whispering in your ears
with a tone that seeks to instantly tear you down.

The fire that is inside of you
is yearning to be released.

Let

     it

          out.

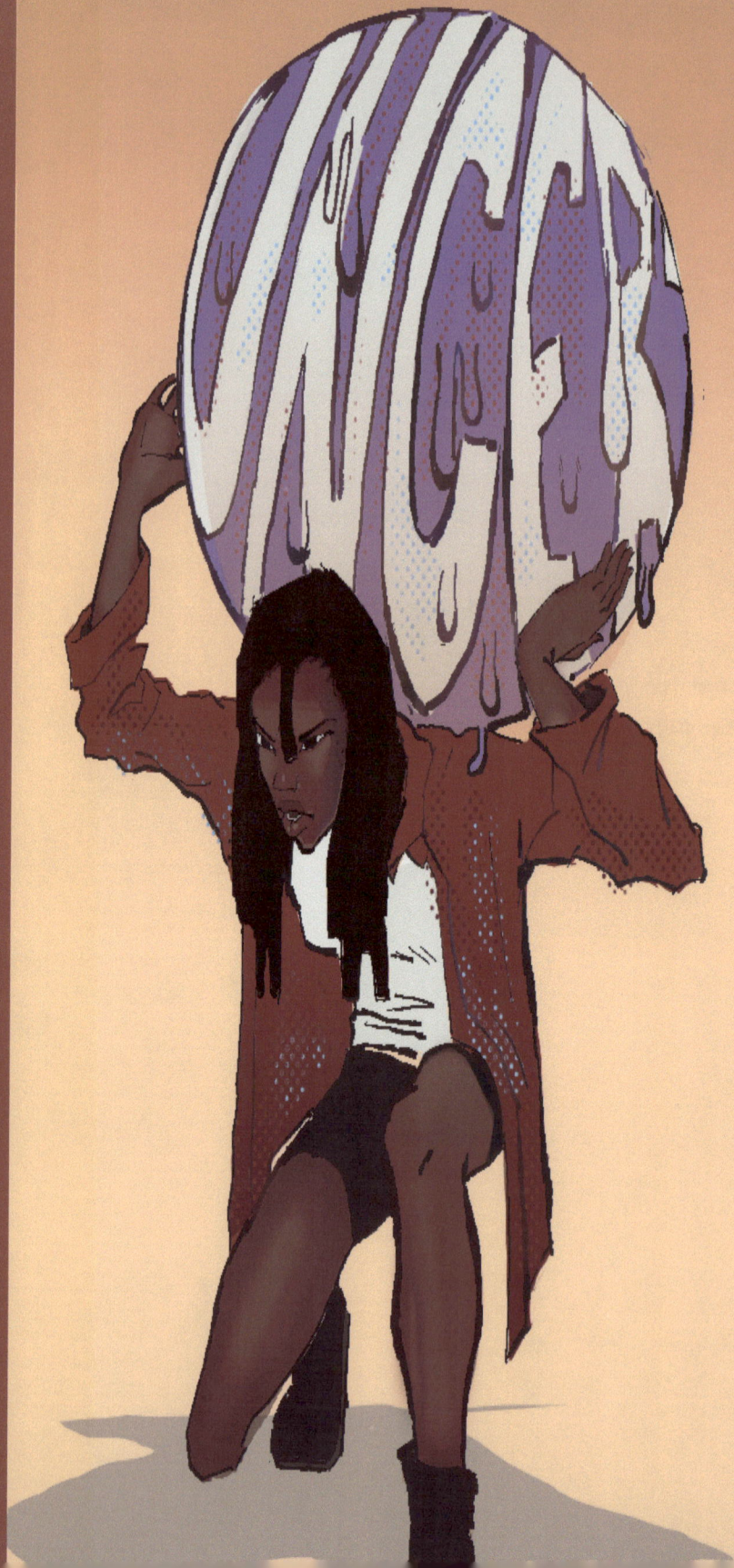

You may have uncertainty
weighing upon your shoulders,
like a boulder,
simply too large for one person to move.

Dear Black Girl, Can We Talk?

WALKER & WALKER
ENTERPRISES

www.lolitawalker.com

2023

OH, *DEAR BLACK GIRL*

You may have anxiousness fluttering in your belly,
like a kaleidoscope of butterflies,
waiting to be unleashed.

Unleashed like a beautiful beast
who will soar higher,
and further and farther
than even you can imagine.

Close your eyes.
Allow the fluttering to take breath
within your beautiful mind.

Dear Black Girl, Can We Talk?

Because you....

You look ahead
and only see obstacles of life
that have mounted before you ....
before me.

Lolita E. Walker

Dear Black Girl,
This is before the world has yet to

see

      your

            greatness.

Dear Black Girl, Can We Talk?

WALKER & WALKER
ENTERPRISES

www.lolitawalker.com
2023

OH,

DEAR

BLACK

GIRL

You may feel fear tugging at your feet,
as you desperately try to forge forward,
in what feels like the thickness of mud
that is unyielding to your attempts.

You may have stood tall as you walked in the room,
then quickly bent back
to dodge the

chatter,
      injustice,
            unequal pay,
                    hurt,
and countless other daggers
that have been lodged your way.

Dear Black Girl, Can We Talk?

WALKER & WALKER
ENTERPRISES

www.lolitawalker.com

2023

BUT, OH *DEAR BLACK GIRL,*

YOU
DID
NOT
FALL

You may be tired,
as you hear another black and brown life taken,
taunted,
belittled,
or unrecognized,
in and around your space.

Dear Black Girl, Can We Talk?

WALKER & WALKER
ENTERPRISES

www.lolitawalker.com

2023

YOU GAIN **STRENGTH** FROM YOUR **FAITH**!

YOUR ANCESTORS WILL CONTINUE TO **LIFT** YOU **HIGHER**!

Oh, *Dear Black Girl,*

I've stopped by today to let you know
that you ...

You are beautiful.

You are armored in God's grace
and you are infused
with the strength of generations before you.

Your chocolate skin emits a brilliant radiance
like no other.

Dear Black Girl, Can We Talk?

WALKER & WALKER
ENTERPRISES

www.lolitawalker.com

2023

CAN YOU SEE IT?

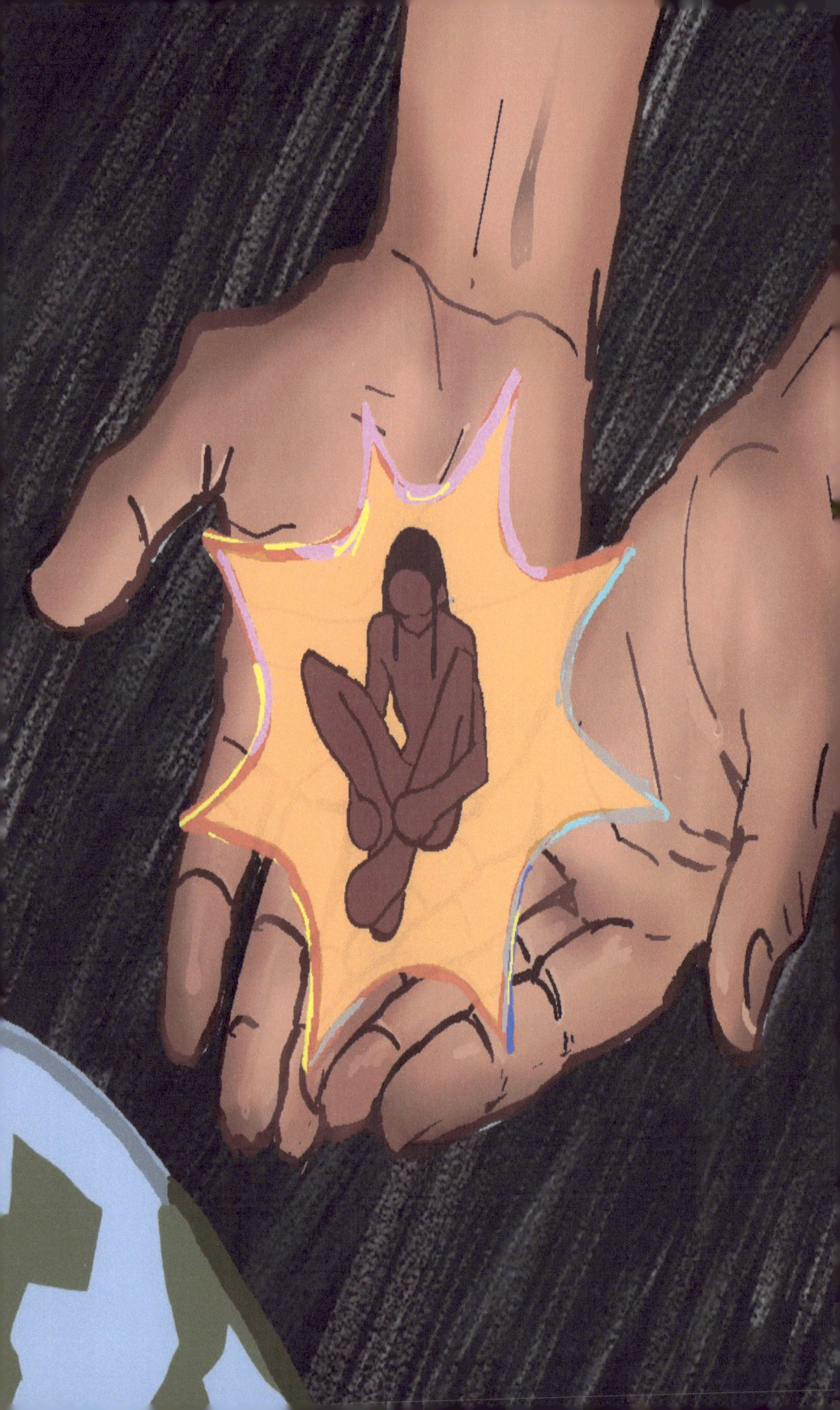

Oh, *Dear Black Girl,*
you are dazzling,
one of God's special gifts to this world.

May you always be reminded
that you,

YES, YOU,

You shine brighter than any diamond,
even after it has been polished anew.

Be reminded that

You
      Are
            Worthy

of surrounding yourself with the support of a tribe,
who will quickly notice
when your cup is inching toward empty,
then rush to help you fill it up.

Oh, *Dear Black Girl,*

please understand that your community
acts as a defense,

who recognizes,
believes,
and knows

that you are strength,
beyond what anyone can say
or what anyone has yet to see,

INCLUDING YOU.

Dear Black Girl, Can We Talk?

WALKER & WALKER
ENTERPRISES

www.lolitawalker.com

2023

DEAR BLACK GIRL,

I WILL HELP

YOU

CARRY YOUR LOAD,

YOU NEED

ONLY ASK!

You are brilliant
beyond where others
may try to set a boundary around you.

You are greatness,
beyond where even you can see.

Dear Black Girl, Can We Talk?

www.lolitawalker.com
2023

DREAM
BIGGER
IN YOUR BETTERMENT.

WALK
TALLER
IN YOUR BOLDNESS.

Oh, *Dear Black Girl,*

I want you to know that YOU,
You are the manifestation of greatness,
right where you stand,
in this very moment.

The indescribable power that lay within you is
PURE MAGIC!

May you set your eyes
beyond where they can see today.

May you know
that there are endless possibilities within you,
simply waiting to be unleashed.

May you know that you are special.
You are enough.
You are light.

Keep shining for the world to see.

AND

If for some reason,
any reason at all,
you find yourself in doubt,
uncertainty,
and/or fear,
may you look in a mirror
and say these words aloud....

**There is power in my voice
and my voice has power.**

This time,
please believe it,
know it,
trust it.

OH, *DEAR BLACK GIRL,* CAN WE TALK?

You are me and I am you!
You are power, passion, and purpose.
May you always be free, live free, and love free.

May you
be you.
for you.
by you.

www.lolitawalker.com
2023

OH, *DEAR BLACK GIRL,* CAN WE TALK?

This is to you to me.
I love you.

(insert your name)

Dear Black Girl, Can We Talk?

www.lolitawalker.com

2023

**TAKE A MOMENT
TO TAKE THREE DEEP BREATHS.**

SOUL WORK

When you feel ready, the next few pages offer a dedicated space for you to journal.

I encourage you to explore what is in your thoughts and on your mind. Some readers may feel a bit shaken, some may find joy and comfort within the words, and others may choose to read and reread the poem to better receive the words, images, and discovery.

A fun fact is that I listen to the audiobook version of this poem as a night-time meditation. The words, coupled with the music, bring me a spirit of peace and a much-needed affirmation that *"Dear Black Girl,"* you will get through this the same way you have every other obstacle set before you. You will find the audiobook of *"Can We Talk? Letters & Poems to Reclaim a Bolder You"* at your favorite streaming location.

Why journal?

Journaling has been proven to help release the feelings and emotions within you. It can be a great tool to improve your mental health, develop yourself personally and reflect on what is happening in your school, work, home, or life.

Journaling has also been known to be one of the many ways to help to manage stress and grow yourself personally. To think more clearly, reduce stress, increase self-confidence, enhance self-awareness, improve your capacity to solve problems, and consider alternative viewpoints, are all documented outcomes of journaling.

Here's your opportunity to engage in a bit of soul work, via journaling.

1. In this moment, after reading the book and experiencing *"Dear Black Girl,"* I feel ...

_____

_____

_____

_____

_____

_____

_____

2. I remember a time when I felt that I needed to be encouraged or to encourage a *"Dear Black Girl."* Write about that time and what you felt in that moment ...

_____

_____

_____

_____

_____

_____

_____

_____

_____

_____

_____

3. **The stanza of the poem that resonated with me the most was …**

_____

_____

_____

_____

_____

4. **The reason that this stanza stood out to me the most was that…**

_____

_____

_____

_____

5. **The illustration within the poem that resonated with me the most was …**

_____

_____

_____

_____

6. **The reason that this illustration resonated with me the most was because …**

_____

_____

_____

_____

7. **If I were to begin to craft a new narrative for my Dear Black Girl, I would say ....**

Dear Black Girl, _____

_____

_____

_____

_____

_____

_____

_____

_____

_____

_____

_____

_____

_____

_____

_____

_____

_____

_____

_____

_____

_____

_____

8. When I choose to embrace my *"Dear Black Girl,"* I am so proud of her. Now that I have completed my soul-work and have looked back at my responses, I realize that at this moment, I feel ....

_____

_____

_____

_____

_____

_____

9. When I find myself speaking negatively to myself, I will

_____

_____

_____

_____

_____

10. When I see another *Dear Black Girl,* I will ....

_____

_____

_____

_____

_____

11. A short list of amazing *Dear Black Girls* in my life are:

- **Name:** _____
- **One thing that makes this *Dear Black Girl* amazing:**

  _____

- **Name:** _____
- **One thing that makes this *Dear Black Girl* amazing:**

  _____

- **Name:** _____
- **One thing that makes this *Dear Black Girl* amazing:**

  _____

- **Name:** _____
- **One thing that makes this *Dear Black Girl* amazing:**

  _____

- **Name:** _____
- **One thing that makes this *Dear Black Girl* amazing:**

  _____

By (insert date) _____, I will individually share what I wrote with each of the *Dear Black Girls* listed above.

COLORING PAGE

In your quiet moments, enjoy a space to color a sketch by Illustrator, Aspen Walker.

THE ENDING

Whether for inspiration, motivation, or reassessment, I pray that my words, illustrations, and soul work were able to meet you where you are, help you pause for a bit, and assist you in unlocking the *"Dear Anxiousness"* within you.

I invite you to visit https://www.lolitawalker.com to stay updated on new books to the *"Can We Talk"* series, services, and products that can help to lift you higher. Please always remember that you are the greatness that others may have yet to see. Remember to see the greatness in yourself! **I do!**

Thank you for trusting me on your journey.

Lolita

THE AUTHOR

Lolita E. Walker is a sought-after, thought leader, ICF professional certified life, leadership, and executive coach, and keynote speaker at the forefront of a movement that empowers busy women and high-powered organizations to feel and trust the power in their pause, reduce overwhelm, and move distractions to achieve un-deniable results, NOW. After leading in the corporate space for nearly twenty years, Lolita founded her personal and professional coaching and consultancy, Walker & Walker Enterprises –

https://www.lolitawalker.com

A mommy of one son, Lolita's superpower is that she up-levels you through "spoken word gospel" to your mind, with the uncanny ability to pull the leadership and greatness that is hidden within. She is a business owner, author of The Intersection of You & Change, podcast host of Coaching, Cocktails & Conversations, a retreat cultivator, and change champion for YOU. Courses, 1:1 and group coaching, personalized affirmations, apparel, and positive products, are only some of the complements to her public speaking and coaching practice.

Lolita graduated from Morgan State University as an Industrial Engineer and Simmons College as a Master's in Business Administration. She is a Ph.D. student, an active member of Alpha Kappa Alpha Sorority, Incorporated, and holds leadership positions in several organizations. She's been where you are and has gotten where you seek to be, in a renewed state of being. The benefit of having a partner who has reached the finish line successfully and systematically, is knowing that her methodologies are the enablers to help you and your teams soar beyond where they stand today.

Can we talk? https://www.lolitawalker.com.

Dear Black Girl, Can We Talk?

WALKER & WALKER
ENTERPRISES

www.lolitawalker.com

2023

A Reflection
From
The Illustrator

As the illustrator of "Dear Black Girl," I attempted to capture the innocence of the everyday Black girl as she navigates through this tough world. As a Black girl myself, I've experienced many of the same difficulties that the girl in the poem experienced. I've looked at myself in the mirror and questioned my worth, despite being wonderfully made by God in His image.

There were times I was thrown into deep thought contemplating how I would conquer the next obstacle that came my way because of my color. I've heard similar stories from other young Black girls throughout my life about what it's like growing up with melanin in certain circumstances. Though stories may differ from girl to girl, woman to woman, we all share a commonality that we may not recognize in the moment -- we overcame. We overcame the whispers, the injustice, the chatter, and the microaggressions. We overcame the hurdles and the obstacles. We can even sit down at times and share a smile, as we shake our heads at the ridiculous encounters we've had throughout our lives.

In this poem, I wanted to be able to capture those moments we, as Black girls, face in this world we live in, but then, express the victorious triumph that makes us the beautiful, strong, and graceful women we are or will become. I want every Black girl to read this poem and know they are amazing and to know that any harsh talk or chatter toward them is only that, and far from the truth. I want them to know they are beyond beautiful and so is their beautiful brown skin. They are so intelligent and capable of anything they put their mind to. I want them to know they are, as the poem says, "armored in God's grace" and so dearly loved beyond what they can possibly comprehend.

Dear Black Girl, I want you to know and believe that you are perfect just the way you are.

-Aspen Walker

BEHIND THE BOOK

"I am such a burden." "I am so stupid." These were two of the phrases that I remember my 89-years young Grandma Bea speaking from her lips. As she said these negative thoughts aloud, I remember thinking about how someone who has been so impactful on this earth could possibly think that these words held any truth. When I asked Grandma Bea if she believed what she was saying, she looked me in my eyes and replied with a simple – yes.

It hurt me to my core.

I remember, at that moment, calling her my *Dear Black Girl* and sharing with her that she is a child of God who is uniquely made. I reminded her that throughout her life, there were times when things seemed so difficult that she thought that she could not get through, yet she had persevered and is standing here to tell the story. I reminded her that she lived through segregation to now see her nieces, nephews, grandchildren, and great-grandchildren as Black business owners, lawyers, judges, teachers, poets, authors, musicians, artists, and even more. I reminded Grandma Beat that she is an amazingness of greatness and that she is a gift to this world.

I had so many emotions and thoughts that filled my mind and my soul as a result of that conversation. They were bubbling inside of me and desperately wanted to get out so I began to write. What resulted from my writing was the poem, *"Dear Black Girl,"* which I published in my second book, *Can We Talk: Letters & Poems to Reclaim a Bolder You.* As I read the words to Grandma Bea that next morning, I remember her smile and her response of how beautiful my words made her feel. I remember her asking me to print it out so that she could read it whenever she wanted. This poem became her daily affirmation. I still read it to her today, at 92 years young. I am so excited to share with her the illustrations from her great-granddaughter, alongside the words of her granddaughter. What an amazing feeling it will be to share with my, *Dear Black Girl.*

If Grandma Bea, after so many years and so many accomplishments could believe the words that she spoke, I knew that there were others who thought the same, whether young or older. There were other *Dear Black Girls* all over the world who needed affirmations that could power them with daily reminders that they were greatness.

This book is number two in a series of many to come.

Please visit https://www.lolitawalker.com for the links to purchase more.

I cannot wait to read your 5-star review of this book, my other books, and my podcast, *Coaching, Cocktails & Conversations*.

Book 1 in the series is called, *"Dear Anxiousness, Can We Talk?"* The next book in the series is called, *"Dear Ancestors, Can We Talk?"* Both books are illustrated by 17-year old artists and I could not be more proud.

THE ACKNOWLEDGEMENTS

To my Heavenly Father and the Lord of my life, *Jesus Christ*. My strength, my encouragement, my light when darkness threatens to cloud my mind, and my compass when I lose my way on my path forward. Your presence, direction, and unconditional love are deeply and humbly appreciated and revered. Thank you.

To Aspen, my niece, and superstar illustrator. May the completion of this book be a reminder that you are greatness and that your art has the power to share emotions that words are unable to speak aloud. Thank you for saying yes to interpreting my words into pictures and your pictures with the world. I pray for increased abundance and publications for years to come. To my son, *Walker*, who is also an amazing artist, yet doesn't quite realize how powerful he is; I pray that you find what lights up your life and then soar in ways unimaginable. I am here to help you on your journey. To my mommy, *Evelyn*, who is a Black girl who supports the world on her shoulders, I pray that this book reminds you that you are worthy of nourishing yourself first. Thank you for being the footstool that helps me to stand afloat. Thank you for supporting my dreams. To my brother, *James-Douglas (JD)*, the father of my creative niece, who helped to push and encourage her when her motivation may have been withering. I appreciate your calming demeanor and your encouragement from across the ways. To **Dr. Juanita Miller,** who said yes to penning the foreword of this book, you, My *Dear Black Girl*, have faced many challenges on your journey, some of which I am unsure that I would have had the energy or drive to leap beyond. I thank you for not only saying yes, but I thank you for your strength, perseverance, and determination. You light up the room with your presence and then create a clear path with your passion. Thank you for your friendship and for the example of what it means to be a resilient *Dear Black Girl.*

Finally, to my father, **Emanuel A. Walker**, my heartbeat that no longer beats, yet still challenges me daily. You were and are, by far, my biggest cheerleader, on and beyond this earth. May you forever be proud of the energy I put into this world. May you smile ear to ear, knowing that the lessons you instilled in me continue to nourish the world in so many ways.

This a reminder to each of you reading and who have listened to this poem, *Dear Black Girl,* in my audiobook, *"Can We Talk? Letters & Poems to Reclaim a Bolder You,"* particularly **my clients and customers** who have trusted me on your individual and collective journeys; I appreciate you and would not be here without you. Your support, encouragement, prayers, and love mean the world to me. Thank you.

My company stands on the foundation of the two strongest pillars of change in my life - my father, last name Walker, and son, first name Walker. I stand at the forefront of our enterprise.

W&W

WALKER & WALKER
E N T E R P R I S E S

....

www.lolitawalker.com

2023

THE BONUS: 10 Affirmations to Power You

Affirmations are declarations to you, by you. To purchase your set of personalized affirmations, please visit lolitawalker.com/shop.

1. Are you doubting yourself and what you bring to the table?
I AM AN AFFIRMER OF MY GIFTS AND ACT IN MY STRENGTHS EACH DAY

2. Do you feel stagnant and as if you are unable to move beyond where you are today?
I AM A BEAUTIFUL COLORED BUTTERFLY AND WILL USE MY WINGS TO SOAR TO EVEN GREATER HEIGHTS

3. Are you giving so much of you to everyone else and rarely taking time to give that same energy back to yourself?
I AM A RESPECTER OF MY TIME AND WILL INTENTIONALLY TAKE MOMENTS FOR ME

4. Do you find yourself stuck in the normalcy of your day-to-day routine?
I ALLOW MYSELF SPACE TO EXPERIENCE THE UNEXPECTED

5. Have you known you are ready to leap, however fear handcuffs your next steps?
I AM ARMED TO FACE MY FEAR AND DARE THEM TO STOP MY JOY

6. Are you finding yourself distracted, working too much, or giving too much energy to those things that are not of the most important?

I AM DISTRACTION FREE AND FIND TIME TO LOVE AND INVEST IN MYSELF

7. Are you overwhelmed with a feeling that chaos surrounds you?

I AM A VISIONARY OF SPACE WHO IMAGINES OPENNESS & TRANQUILITY

8. Are your thoughts moving quickly and your actions and reactions happening just as quickly?

I AM IN TOUCH WITH MY THOUGHTS AND MINDFUL OF MY ACTIONS

9. Do you find yourself not speaking up at work, in meetings, at home? Do you sometimes think it will be easier if you didn't say anything? Do you occasionally feel powerless?

I AM INTENTIONALLY AFFIRMING MY POWER BY GIVING IT MY VOICE AND I AM AFFIRMING MY VOICE BY GIVING IT MY POWER

10. Are you holding on to something that is not sitting right with your spirit?

I AM THE NOURISHMENT FOR MY SOUL, SO I WILL FORGIVE MYSELF FIRST.

Authors Note: There may be a number of these scenarios or even a single affirmation that resonates with you the most. That is perfectly normal. Here's a thought that I use with my clients: Say those particular affirmations aloud for 7 days. At the end of your affirmations, say, "I AM (INSERT YOUR FIRST, MIDDLE, AND LAST NAME)" If you'd like to say a combination that resonates with you, have fun and be intentional with your words and your actions!

Notes & Reflections

_____

_____

_____

_____

_____

_____

_____

_____

_____

_____

_____

_____

_____

_____

_____

_____

_____

_____

_____

_____

_____

_____

_____

Notes & Reflections

Notes & Reflections

_____

_____

_____

_____

_____

_____

_____

_____

_____

_____

_____

_____

_____

_____

_____

_____

_____

_____

_____

_____

Notes & Reflections

Dear Black Girl, Can We Talk?

WALKER & WALKER
ENTERPRISES

www.lolitawalker.com
2023

Dear Black Girl,

Can We Talk?

WALKER & WALKER
E N T E R P R I S E S

....

www.lolitawalker.com

2023

www.ingramcontent.com/pod-product-compliance
Lightning Source LLC
Chambersburg PA
CBHW040939100426

42812CB00015B/2624